We Lit the Lamps Ourselves
ANDREA POTOS

salmonpoetry

Published in 2012 by
Salmon Poetry
Cliffs of Moher, County Clare, Ireland
Website: www.salmonpoetry.com
Email: info@salmonpoetry.com

Copyright © Andrea Potos, 2012

ISBN 978-1-907056-92-5

All rights reserved. No part of this publication may be reproduced or transmitted in any form or by any means, electronic or mechanical, including photography, recording, or any information storage or retrieval system, without permission in writing from the publisher. The book is sold subject to the condition that it shall not, by way of trade or otherwise, be lent, resold or otherwise circulated without the publisher's prior consent in any form of binding or cover other than that in which it is published and without a similar condition, including this condition, being imposed on the subsequent purchaser.

COVER ARTWORK: © *Melissad10* | *Dreamstime.com*
COVER DESIGN: *Siobhán Hutson*

The Poets light but Lamps –
Themselves – go out –
The Wicks they stimulate –
If vital Light

Inhere as do the Suns –
Each Age a Lens
Disseminating their
Circumference –

EMILY DICKINSON

*

Sitting among the heather,
Suddenly I saw
That all the moor was alive!...
And having seen, knew all...

from "Heirloom" by KATHLEEN RAINE

Acknowledgements

Acknowledgments are due to the editors of the following, in which some of the poems from this collection first appeared:

Emily, Dying – *The Comstock Review*, 2nd place, Muriel Craft Bailey Award

The Lost Sisters – *Sou'wester*

Ellen Nussey, After Charlotte's Death – *Phoebe: A Journal of Feminist Scholarship*

Opening the Brontë Biography
Emily, Dying – *The Brontë Society Gazette*

To Emily Brontë
On Haworth Moor
Two Emilys
Morning Writing Practice
To Dorothy Wordsworth
Questions for Lavinia Dickinson – *Poetry East*

Morning Writing Practice – also appeared in chapbook, *Abundance to Share With the Bird*s (Finishing Line Press)

To the College Girl Who Sold. . . – *North American Review*

Leaving the Brontës
Biographical Notice of Emily Brontë – *Poetry Salzburg Review*

On the Moors
Charlotte Brontë, Student
Charlotte Brontë Speaks of Poet Laureate Robert Southey, 1837
At the Mall Cineplex
At the Meeting of the Waters
Charlotte Brontë as Governess – *Women's Review of Books*

Emily's List
Charlotte's Diary
Beginning Jane Eyre – *Green Mountains Review*

Charlotte at the Sea – *Cairn*

The Brontë Skirt – *Prairie Schooner*

Applied Literature
Finally, the Poem is Done – *Main Street Rag*

Waiting – *Poetry Jumps Off the Shelf* program, Woodrow Hall Editions
To Be Near Emily – *Blue Unicorn*
Emily Dickinson Stays Home. . . – *Nimrod International Journal*
Women Poets Before Me – *Not a Muse Anthology* (Haven Books)

Contents

PART ONE

To Emily Brontë	11
The Brontë Skirt	12
Speaking of Poetry	13
Being Emily Dickinson	14
To the College Girl Who Sold *The Life of Emily Dickinson*	15
Opening the Brontë Biography	16
On the Moors	17
The Lost Sisters	18
The Tiny Books	19
At the Meeting of the Waters	20
Emily's Homesickness	21
Charlotte Brontë, Student	22
The Walking	23
Charlotte Brontë as Governess	24
Emily's List	25
Two Emilys	26
A Fairer House	27
Publishing the Book of Rhymes	28
Beginning *Jane Eyre*	29
Family Portrait by Branwell Brontë	30
Emily, Dying	31
Charlotte Speaks of Anne	32
Charlotte's Diary	33
Emily Dickinson Stays Home When Ralph Waldo Emerson Visits Her Brother's House	34
Charlotte Brontë Speaks of Poet Laureate Robert Southey, 1837	35
Waiting	36
Mrs. Gaskell Speaks of the Woman Artist	37
From the Notebooks of Emily Carr	38
To Dorothy Wordsworth	41

PART TWO

The Brontës' Blood	45
Finally, the Poem is Done	46
Morning Writing Practice	47
To Be Near Emily	48
Biographical Notice of Emily Brontë	49
George Richmond's Portrait of Charlotte, 1850	51
Charlotte at the Sea	52
Charlotte's Response to a Reader, 1850	53
Ellen Nussey, After Charlotte's Death, 1856	54
On Haworth Moor	55
Shouting *Heathcliff* on the Moors	56
Leaving the Brontës	57
Sylvia Plath at Wuthering Heights	58
When Sylvia Takes Up Her Pen	59
Sylvia and the Daffodils	60
Found on Sylvia's Desk	61
Questions for Lavinia Dickinson	62
A Visitor to Haworth Parsonage	63
Rendezvous With Light	64
Applied Literature	65
At the Gym With the Brontës	66
At the Mall Cineplex	67
After Writing the Poem	68
This Morning is Not a Poem	69
Emily Dickinson and Emily Brontë	70
Women Poets Before Me	71
About the author	73

PART ONE

TO EMILY BRONTË

Eleven years old and sunk in the red velveteen
chair at the Fox Bay Theater, I absorbed
the raw sculpture of Penistone Crag,
bracken and gorse, the peat
blanketing the Yorkshire moors. Heathcliff
with his sea-green eyes, black cape swirled
around him, how tall and alarmingly
handsome he looked.
At Catherine's grave he cried, you wrote:
I cannot live without my life,
desire held hostage in his eyes,

my heart held stunned in my chest.
Years later, I return to your words;
travel to the stone-
flagged floors of your home;
your desk-box saved under glass,
its lining worn, purple velvet
splotched with red sealing wax.
Walking the rocky footpath towards swells
of purple heather, I remember the words
of the local stationer who saw you
returning one evening: *her countenance was lit up
by a divine light*. I imagine
I hear your skin
brush mine, whisper what you know:
the silence, the stars
that burn through the page.
Hone the hours to their core—you might have said—
wind and poem, passion and moor.

THE BRONTË SKIRT

I found it pressed between the sweaters, outside
on the sale rack of the import store:
three tiers of sun-faded cloth
substantial as parlor drapery—
crushed velour and cotton
dressed with mauve ruffles and, here and there,
the embroidered emblems of a forgotten time
from those novels I devoured as a girl:
Little Women, Jane Eyre, a skirt I imagine
19th century women wore—the Brontë sisters
as they climbed the steep cobbles of Main Street,
returning from the stationer or the apothecary
with bundles in their arms for Papa and themselves,
as they traipsed across Haworth Moor,
the potent depth of peat under them,
curlews shrieking and swooping over their heads
and winds wrapping around them like shawls.
Their skirts swept freely over bracken and gorse,
skirts with a weight, a sureness of their own,
the presence of something more than myself
I long to wear.

SPEAKING OF POETRY

She said there's a clarity in each word,
like the chandelier
that hung in your dining room as a child—
stars of blue-white and yellow-gold,
even purple and magenta could be found
sparking on all the walls;
each piece of the chandelier—
a teardrop whole and dipped in light—
you could see your whole life through it.

BEING EMILY DICKINSON

The white dress is easy enough,
the desk tucked at the window;
paper, ink, silence
as the house bows to sleep.

What of the heft
and breadth of Lexicon—
the soul at whitest heat,
the *unannointed Blaze*—

     to dwell on pristine
dunes of mind, each wind-
lashed grain afire—

     who could bear such brightness?

TO THE COLLEGE GIRL WHO SOLD
THE LIFE OF EMILY DICKINSON

What can I say to you, twenty years after
you carried the two-volume,
hardcover first edition with illustrations
through the musty portal
of the used bookstore, as if it were
an average day.

Hungry for cash,
you couldn't wait
to unload the books from your pack,
this one gift from your father
when you were a girl of thirteen
dreaming yourself a poet
at your white wooden desk.

How did the years convince you
ten dollars pouring through your fingers—
a bottle of Chianti for that night
and what is long forgotten—surpassed

Awe, the vision
of the woman, the soul at white heat

          infinite Circumference of a Life
you'd be craving one day.

OPENING THE BRONTË BIOGRAPHY

With my child barely asleep, I tiptoe
to my room, my chaise lounge
that all day has laid empty.
Forgetting the phone, the bell,
the dishwasher's gurgle and churn downstairs,

I take the story into my hands.
I step on a smooth sandstone floor,
see windows without curtains,
a bare vista of graves, beyond them—fields
like unfettered paths of the mind.

I hear the chop of knives,
smell the browning of bread
and apple pudding.

    Women's voices wind in
from the back kitchen.
    My breath rises to meet them.

   On the cold stairwell,
a grandfather clock resounds
another forgotten,
startling hour.

ON THE MOORS, The Brontës

Some shun it here—
call it tree-starved, stunted,
drizzled in mist.

In untrammeled air, curlews cry.
Over bilberry, gorse,
spikes of purple heather,
the earth is a bog that erupted one day–
under blackened skies, peat and mud flowed for miles,
swept away bridges, suffocated fish.
> (Papa preached that God unsheathed
> his sword, brandished it over our heads.
> *Be thankful we are spared*, he cried.)

Indeed, this ground is a living being
that breathes through our soles,

the air
an infinite undone page,
the wind the voice that dictates.

THE LOST SISTERS

The elder Brontë sisters, Maria and Elizabeth, died of tuberculosis at ages 11 and 10, in Haworth, England, 1825.

At the Clergy Daughter's School,
we breathed the chill that brought our death,
our chests becoming stone.

We left our sisters
with the burden
of Mind–
lands, faces beyond
washing draped over the lane wall to dry,
the iron's hiss on our father's collars,
the housekeeper's call to supper.

We buried ourselves in the pages
of their hearts–

we could not bear
the keening of the lover sweeping through our dreams,
the lonesome girl shivering and coughing in her cot;

we foresaw the woman
turning the bed to flame.

THE TINY BOOKS, Charlotte Brontë

The Brontë children created miniscule-sized, hand-stitched books, filling them with wild adventure stories.

We grabbed scraps from sugar bags,
parcel wrappings, wallpaper.
With a scientist's precision, we bent
to our task—
our printing became the code
impossible for adults.

Papa's gift of toy soldiers led us
to our Glasstown, our Angria.
Conquest, riches and revolution ruled the hours—
the grand Duke of Wellington,
Ross and Percy returned from their expeditions,
even the evil Bonaparte.

Startling, dark Zamorna loomed through my mind.

No matter that we were called
to scrub the potatoes,
sweep the rugs and floors,

inside our dailiness dwelled marble palaces,
battlefields, such *thrones of pure and massive gold*.

AT THE MEETING OF THE WATERS,
Charlotte

Far over moorland,
beyond the daily ramble
is the place that belongs
to Emily and Anne. They call it
the Meeting of the Waters.
They lead me there one morning,
to turf the hue
and sheen of emeralds.
Delicate springs suprise me,
play such light music over stones.

Larger stones offer us rest
for the hours we dwell where
only the sky knows us,
and clear waters rise
from their source.

It is here Emily proclaims:
I'll walk where my own nature
would be leading,
*It vexes me to choose
another guide*, her voice
swept and lost
over miles of windtossed heather.

EMILY'S HOMESICKNESS

> *After three months with Charlotte at the Roe Head School,*
> *Emily returned to Haworth parsonage and her moors, 1835.*

Charlotte saw her sunken eyes, whitened cheeks,
the wasting frame:
No one knew
what ailed her but me.

Oh, not to be pinned
by the ringing of the bell,
nailed to the chair
for French, German,
geography!
        No one but she
        knew Eden's location–

in the kitchen with Tabby,
peeling the day's potatoes, kneading the bread,
sweeping the floors,

        roaming beyond the windows and graves,
where roses shot up in the blackest of heath
and the purple heather bloomed her name.

CHARLOTTE BRONTË, STUDENT

Roe Head School, 1831

When I arrived, they eyed me queerly,
these daughters of wealthy locals.
Oh, I could not blame them—me with
spectacles and old woman's dress,
unmistakable tinge of Irish on my tongue.

I offered them poetry, my zeal
for drawing, those subjects most females
are not given to learn:
geography, history, grammar,
French verbs;
such copious, joyful copying
of classical heads and hands!

Papa says I must meet my future armed.
I memorize Mangall's *Historical*
and Miscellaneous Questions, for it is the latter
that calls to me—
what we are not given to know,
what cannot be reduced—
woman's mind
bursting the bounds of breads and puddings,
of embroidering collars and bags.

THE WALKING

> "*The sisters maintained their evening ritual of walking in the parlour...*"
>
> BRIAN WILKS, *The Brontës*

Their father's fear of fire
makes carpet forbidden,
they walk on bare stone.
Some would call it pacing,
this circling
the dining room table each night.
They link arms,
tread this space
(the way by heart),

reciting passages,
plotting future chapters
of their tales, the hours
of eventless days.
At the steep top of a cobbled street,
in this high moor parish where wind
and storm reach them,
their footsteps intone the bond.

CHARLOTTE BRONTË AS GOVERNESS

It is true I've said
a private governess has no
existence beyond the weary, unending lessons;
unruly children; commands
from those who fail to see
her true face. They thrust upon her
oceans of needlework and mending.

Yet, on certain days, I know
my heart beats in my breast.
My mind roams unblighted
out of the nursery,
travels to places strange–
the attic room we found
on our visit to the Ripon manor house.
      Behind a tall tapestry was stashed
a secret room where not one window
hinted toward another life.

Scorched beams, cracked walls,
an iron cot rusted
and hunched in the corner
caused me to shiver, rumors
of a mad woman once
tucked under those eaves,
behind battlements
like admonitions to the world.

EMILY'S LIST

> *"She was not the first woman to find domestic occupations sat well with creative writing..."*
>
> Robert Barnard, *Emily Brontë*

Make the beds,
keep Tiger and Jasper
off the counterpanes.
Help Sally with the washing,
scrub front flagstones,
dining room fender.
Pick black currants with Anne,
walk on the moor before tea.
(Find the tadpole pool,
the linnet's nest.)
Peel apples for Tabby's pudding.
Read to Papa.
Walk once more,
in dusk,
open copybook–
*(Winds take a pensive tone,
stars a tender fire).*

TWO EMILYS

Who can say what happens
to a woman alone in her room,
with sheer white drapes trembling in air
rushing invisibly over her letters to the world,

or, when she leaves the walls behind her,
deskbox propped under arm,
mastiff sniffing the ground at her side,
the fierce countenance of the crags,
the wind's holler making translations in her body.

A FAIRER HOUSE

> *"When a census taken in 1870 listed Emily Dickinson's occupation, it used the phrase employed for dependent daughters: without occupation."*
>   JUDITH FARR

They did not note my
conservatory lilies,
my jasmines,
or my rye and Indian bread
that keeps my father glad.

They had no eyes
to see
Possibility
where I work—
their houses such prose.

Within these red brick walls,
their feet
would not follow
Me—past
the mazes of Real
        into undulating tunnels

of the Infinite's ear—our voices
to one another   echo
answer—

PUBLISHING THE BOOK OF RHYMES, Charlotte, 1846

Once Emily's rage subsided
(I'd read her startling poems
without permission),
I convinced my sisters both
and began with a vigor
unmatched in recent weeks.

Aylott & Jones, No. 8,
Paternoster Row, London
agreed to aid us.
We agreed, of course,
to bear the risk.

We set to work eagerly,
watched for the post each day,
corrected errors from memory
(surely, a proofreader should know stars
tremble, not *tumble*).

We suspected authoresses to be
pitied, babied, even
flattered with false praise;
we did what we would–ushered ourselves
into the world
behind the veils of *Currer*,
Acton, *Ellis*.

BEGINNING *JANE EYRE*

Here, in this narrow,
red-brick Manchester residence,
Papa is on his back in a darkened room,
bandages over his eyes.
For five weeks I must abide, while he lies still.
May Divine Mercy grant him
restoration of sight.

At home, Emily and Anne keep house,
Branwell declines in drink.
A toothache rages me awake most nights.
In place of sleep, I have desk-box, pencil,
my square paper books
I must hold close to my face.
I record an orphaned girl in a window seat
on a lamentable November day,
Bewick's History of British Birds on her lap.
     See how she is drawn to the pictures
of windswept sea-fowl, billow and spray,
infinite reservoirs of frost and snow,
rock and promontory,
death-white realms I know
so strangely as my own.

FAMILY PORTRAIT BY BRANWELL BRONTË

There is no evidence of joy
in these straight mouths,
curls tight and framing
the three sisters'
alabaster skin;
eyes opened to their fullest reach,
as if seeing
into days that must be borne.

Between Emily and Charlotte,
a pillar-shaped space is lit
by unmistakable absence,
erasure;

the viewer can almost trace the cravat,
the red, bushy hair,
a figure brushed out–
    was it disgust?
   (gambling, drinking, debt),

failed painter, poet whose entreaties
Wordsworth would not answer,

ghostly proof.

EMILY, DYING

> *Refusing all medication and assistance, Emily Brontë died of tuberculosis at age 30.*

Nights, I can hear the worry scraping
in Charlotte's hands;
Father's fear
staining the air.

I tell them I'll have no
poisoning doctor near me,
no tricks of homepathy
let loose in my blood.

This cough corsets my throat;
knives jab at my side when
I breathe.
I follow

where this leads,
just as the Voice
once howled through my pen   spat out
a Man's dark irrepressible heart

so now
no coward soul is mine

     O God within my breast—
the windlashed moors of my body
are cleared for You.

CHARLOTTE SPEAKS OF ANNE

Unlike Emily, she submitted
to care; she swallowed the vegetable balsam,
cod liver oil to soothe
her torn throat.

May warmth only worsened her.
I watched with horror
the past return:
morning lethargy,
evening fever,
a cough
tolling through our walls in the night.

At the end,
she pleaded for the sea.
Lifting her in and out of carriages, trains,
we took her to Scarborough.
She drove on the sands
in a donkey cart.
She rested by the window,
urged me to *Take Courage*.
I followed her gaze that reached out to the sea—
water so smooth, so calm, such a surface
clear enough to pierce a life.

CHARLOTTE'S DIARY

*After the deaths of Branwell, Emily, and Anne.
Winter, 1849*

Evening is the great trial.
Alone in the dining room, I relive
us gathered here with
our books,
our desk-boxes.

Now Papa is closed
behind his study doors.
Emily's dog Keeper
snivels at my feet.

   In place of my sisters, my brother,
only *solitude, remembrance,
longing*,
the stairwell clock ticking

its incessant ignorance
of What Is.

   Never was an emptiness fuller than this.

For *rooted sorrow*, I must turn
toward Imagination—
let my pen stroke the wound.

EMILY DICKINSON STAYS HOME WHEN RALPH WALDO EMERSON VISITS HER BROTHER'S HOUSE

Let there be no argument
from the grass between
my brother's house and mine.
No need to touch flesh–

like the Word, he must glow.
Hadn't we met in that place
where Dream is born–

I remember–Soul sparks
erupted–I felt
my own ignite–
in my ear–*the Mountains straight reply.*

CHARLOTTE BRONTË SPEAKS OF POET LAUREATE ROBERT SOUTHEY, 1837

How I hungered for his reply!
When he informed me I possess
in no inconsiderable degree
the faculty of verse, my hopes
escaped from their cellar, quivered
and peered from the margins.

He warned me of danger: woman's duties
misdirected, forgotten,
a distempered state of mind.
Though I may scribble in the few
idle hours (for nourishment of heart
and soul), let me not embrace
notions of glory—he urged me
to hold to my Destiny:

turning the linen,
gathering the turnips and potatoes,
scrubbing the fireplace fender 'til it shines—
he knows not how (could any man know?) with this pen
how near to the flame I bend.

WAITING

Over a week now and still my Inbox
empty, so that I think
I may as well have hunkered down
at the weathered mahoghany table
in the sitting room, the grandfather clock tolling
quarter hours, an oil lamp or perhaps a candle
flickering its gold across the paper as I dip my pen in
and out of the well, scratching my message
while winds moan beyond rattling windowpanes
and rain lashes down with a fury,
the whole elemental drama accompanying my letter
taking weeks by gig or steam train to reach you,
you breaking the seal,
reading my words as if they matter.

MRS. GASKELL SPEAKS OF THE WOMAN ARTIST

From her biography of Charlotte Brontë, 1857.

When a man becomes author, he may
simply slide out
from his trade, be it grocer,
banker, barrister.

Not so the wife,
mother,
the daughter for whom Home
seizes heart and bone.

When genius falls
upon her, encloses her in its
unrelenting arms,

the woman must iron, sweep,
fill the family's table.
Then she may tiptoe
to her desk-box
while the household sleeps–

She must not hide her gift in a napkin,

she must remember Mary
who bowed to the white
blinding Angel;

she must bow to the word, the God-
appointed pen.

FROM THE NOTEBOOKS OF EMILY CARR

Emily Carr (1871-1945) is considered Canada's most famous woman painter. In her middle age, she became known for her paintings of the forests of British Columbia where she lived. Her journals record her search to express her artistic and spiritual drives in her work.

The winds still bite,
so my trees must wait for me.
I'll hold on to the image from my dream–
positive and negative
colours adjoined:
red-green, blue-orange,
yellow-purple slapping
canvas awake.

Such relief after yesterday
when six pictures came back from Ottawa
without even rejection
or thanks.
Nothing hurts like nothingness–

So what old girl, I tell myself today–
make them your little mound
of manure. Spread it
lavishly around and watch
what grows.

                        *

My visitor stayed too long–
diminuitive talk leaches,
exhausts the very bones.
Does one ever find interior friends?

Even the parson disappointed—
he relished my food, my old pictures,
the ones that barely pierce skin.
He fawned over detail, while
I tried to convey my big canvas—vast pines
soaring through immaculate space,
but he could not see.
Of the totem mother he said
he'd hate to find her
in his dreams.
Pshaw! I can't tell him

how I ache for movement and expanse,
full glory of sky, *the blue
that is so much more than blue.*

*

I looked over my sketches
of last week, shook my head at
their dull paper willfulness.
They are paint, not God.
I must go out and feel more,

ask the woods
what is this vital thing it holds,
this urgent pulse of trees
thrumming a passage through blood—

their sprawling dumb magnificence with
roots unfurling and breathing beneath us—

they tap on my soles until I lean
to listen.

Let me do the daily
in heat and light.

Let me paint with the stillness
that becomes my brush, when
the spoken words remain unspoken.

*

These old bones, rheumatic joints
would stop me if they could.
I must pinch my spirit to get up–back
into that wideness, that liveness I love–

the cliffs where I sketched this evening,
that crimson-saffron sky people gasp over, well,
I'm impatient for it to be done,
I want the moments beyond it–
tender melting mystery–

no raving glare or dark,
just peace
deepening through air
like the soul free to muse
when the body finally sleeps.

TO DOROTHY WORDSWORTH

You found the lone strawberry flower
hidden under the hedge,
heard the far-off becks and falls,
the voice of water in wind.
By moonlight you planted lemon thyme.

Helm Crag, you wrote:
rose very bold. . . a being by itself.
Once, you called yourself *more than half a poet.*

Weren't you the first to tell
of the daffodils tossing and reeling,
the single leaf like a windblown rag?

Though you gladly let fame
crown your brother, beloved brother
who worshipped celestial light on earth.
You baked his bread, prepared supper,
tea for the two of you and Coleridge;

you listened for his tread
upon the evening path, as he
must have waited for the glimpses
from the shooting lights of your wild eyes.

PART TWO

THE BRONTËS' BLOOD

> "... *all writers write in their bodies.*"
>   – GAYLE BRANDEIS

I can't imagine how you did it–
navigated the back garden to the privy
your long skirts skimming the dirt and ice,
rags stuffed in your palms.
How did you keep them in place
as you climbed over the bogs and crags,
or draped linen over stones to dry.

As you circled the candlelit table
reciting passages to each other from your tales,
did you ever stop to ponder
the womanly truth–
breasts, thighs, and sexes
stashed under volumes of rustling cloth.
Charlotte, sole to marry, dying months thereafter,
did you know a child grew in you?
Emily, Anne–did you ever crave
to hold a man?
The blood of creation surged through your hands.

FINALLY, THE POEM IS DONE

and you sigh with the relief
of the woman whose child slips out wet
and living from between her quivering legs
after hours of push and moan,
her body drenched and appalled,
after the rest
which was so simple—blind cell seeking
cell through the arching
river inside her,
communing
at perhaps the moment she turned
to flip on the lamp beside her bed, or
sunk back on her pillow
with a book alight on her belly
listening to the March winds coiling
and shrieking around the corners
of her house, all she needed then
was to prop a pillow
under her, wait with her hips tilted
the way the earth tilts seamlessly and leans
toward summer.

MORNING WRITING PRACTICE

Lately it consists of gazing out
at the lake, at gulls
skittering and grazing
the surface for food

while I pour another thermos cup
of the black tea I brewed
hours ago before my daughter
stirred from her sleep

and construction of the day began,
when the house was still
unmarred water,
before I heard the red enamel pot

singing on top of the stove,
calling me to come, come now,
screeching until
I gave it my whole attention.

TO BE NEAR EMILY

A friend who studied at Amherst
told me about the pilgrims who come
leaving scraps of paper, beads and flowers,
hoping to breathe some rarified air.
He and his friends would wait until
the last one wandered off

before they leaned against the stones
in the dusk. They sprawled their legs
on the graveyard grass and rolled joints,
lit them—tiny lasers to pierce the foggy
distance within, as soberly, was her supreme
and daily task.

BIOGRAPHICAL NOTICE OF EMILY BRONTË
3 voices

1. Charlotte, 1845

One autumn afternoon I lighted upon
a manuscript of verse—
my sister's mouse-sized scrawl,

not the usual trim
clipped borders of a common
woman's heart,

a peculiar music—
nearly inaudible soulcry—
melancholy

euphoric, as if some dormant
wilderness dwelled there
thundering on the door of
the world she had no mind for.

2. Reviewer of Wuthering Heights, 1848

A rugged, brutal power resides here.
Who is this Ellis Bell—male,
female?
Has some Demon
invaded the Yorkshire moors,
traded ink for blood?

Open this book at your risk,
lightening jags each page,
scorches the eyes.

Surely no woman
would conjure such a tale.

3. Emily, 1848

   Moan of the wind Almighty,
     purple high waving heather   *stormy blasts*
bending and torrents raving over rocks where I played.

I was alone
    when wildfire   thundered
through my untouched body–

only heath, crag, hill
    prepared me
        for what I was to bear.

GEORGE RICHMOND'S PORTRAIT OF CHARLOTTE, 1850

My publisher commissioned these
three full days at the artist's studio
near Baker Street, London.
With simple chalk he worked
to create my likeness–
a gift for Papa.

I sat stiff; I would not watch the motion
of his deft hands
capturing such a plain
countenance as mine,
my forehead so broad and bold,
I must mask it with my hair.

How glad I was for the end!
He'd done my grey eyes well,
but, oh, that "swan's neck," those thin
lines forged by artistic invention–
they belonged only to my lost Anne,
and I wept.

CHARLOTTE AT THE SEA

Near Scarborough, 1852

In wind-beaten darkness, during the long
night-vigils, Solitude
seemed Desolation.
Anne's grave was so near (I discovered
five errors inscribed in her stone
and ordered it refaced).

I feared the sea would not suit me.
I began to walk— three, four hours
of each day. The great shore seethed
with turbid waves, sea-birds diving
toward white foam.
The air swelled with a roar deeper
than thunder.
I felt Repair stir
faintly within;

my skin turned weather-struck
and red as an old fisherman,
a bathing woman
rising from the elements
of salt, despair.

CHARLOTTE'S RESPONSE TO A READER, 1850

Your letter brought genial company
to fog-enshrouded hours,
the protest of winds at every window.

*You are very welcome to take Jane,
Caroline and Shirley for your sisters.*
Do not berate your delight
for having your youth as its source–

enjoy your adopted sisters' presence now;
let them soothe a solitary heart,
cool a feverish brow.
Take them on your life's journey
until you need them no more–
    they will not mind

no more than high summer minds
relinquishing to frost,
and sunsteeped day
bows, as it must,
before night's command.

ELLEN NUSSEY, AFTER CHARLOTTE'S DEATH, 1856

> *Charlotte's husband Arthur Bell Nichols was horrified by the revelatory quality of Charlotte's letters to her longtime friend Ellen Nussey. If Ellen did not promise to burn the letters after reading them, he said, he would censor their correspondence.*

Who was he to claim Master
of our intimacy?
He peered over her shoulder,
called our words *Dangerous
as lucifer matches.*
      Oh he roiled a fever in me—
what did he know
of two hearts
forged in girlhood's crucible?

I pledged myself to their destruction.

I saved them all.

Three hundred alone

spark in Mrs. Gaskell's
ready hands.

Forgive me Lord—
      it was my one flight
from duty,
the sure, true lie I gave to the world.

ON HAWORTH MOOR

You follow the Public Footpath sign,
manuever in your Reeboks
over a muddy, cobbled lane.
A wooden arrow blanched by water
and wind points the way.
As you begin, the mist
becomes rain, though it's not as if
it matters; you have waited
since childhood for this, since you first
closed the cover of your Signet classic
edition, since your first matinee at the Fox Bay,
watching Heathcliff loom at you,
the ghosts roaming the bogs and crags;
your Junior Mints untouched on your lap while
you stared at the vastness unrolling,
never believing your own feet would
touch the stones on this path,
that the month would be August, the moors
a glory of purple,
nothing but tiny stars of purple
heather on every side, the hills
sheathed in fog, and you, walking
in a stunned kind of mind as if the dead
were being raised, in solitude
and unbridled air, right now your eyes
could be hers.

SHOUTING *HEATHCLIFF* ON THE MOORS

At last, the Brontë sky of girlhood—

dreamseeped hours within the pages

black and white woodcut drawings becoming

this silver wuthering   hawks curlews

shrieking past crags

and cloudbeasts tumbling and merging

   above my head   my flung-out arms

my long-kept cry returned

to its source.

LEAVING THE BRONTËS

I stand a long time
on the uneven, cobbled lane;
knowing I may never travel
3,000 miles again to see
the white chemise, Emily's sole
remaining clothing (I imagine her
tall body in fragile cotton
only the dimmest light preserves).
And her deskbox with its stained,
purple lining; within it, the letter
from her publisher addressed "Dear Sir,"
discussing a second novel
that will never be known.
I will have to rely on guidebooks
for the proofs they were here—
Charlotte's honeymoon dress, worn nine months
before she died, faded from lavendar
to a brownish mauve that cannot be touched;
the wooden pattens worn over shoes—
on windy, winter nights, how they must
have clattered on the cold stone floors.
And let me always remember those dulled-white gloves
that fit the tiniest of hands,
those circlets of fawn-colored hair—real hair—
braided and strung
into a bracelet, a brooch
intended for those who survive.

SYLVIA PLATH AT WUTHERING HEIGHTS

On your mind's whetstone
you sharpened each thought—
sparks slapped and nipped

the roaring air while you hiked in your woolens
among heath-grass and gorse,
sketchbook poised under your arm.

Your husband wrote: you were *twice as ambitious*
as Emily, and the wind-flogged moors
came with empty eyes to find you.

The shattered mullions flashed,
the wild stones moaned your name.
Beneath your skin, word-arrows quivered   took aim.

WHEN SYLVIA TAKES UP HER PEN

The white page
finds its prism,
its core
of violet,
crimson, blue.

Stones scarred with centuries
careen into streams.
The roots of heather and gorse
invite her in,
near to the one
whose hand she knows.

SYLVIA AND THE DAFFODILS

I like to imagine their one spring
in the Devon countryside: daffodils
by the thousands in their yard
among the apple trees, a Wordsworthian
dream for real—Sylvia enshrined
with her children among blooms
(bunches cut to sell at Market, and still
abundance remains)—lemon yellow,
primrose, canary waving and resplendent
in the gentle air. And Ted on his knees
with the camera. I like to change
the ending of this story—as if the daffodils
could seed within her, the true yellow
could crowd out the bitter wintering
to come, could carry her through.

FOUND ON SYLVIA'S DESK

A sheaf of vellum pages,
each poem

a watermarked secret,
an unsplintered self,

a graven stone,
yew branch pointing up to the moon.

A morning song of tulip,
poppy, blood-seeped

flight into the cauldron and out
into the bare mouth of the spring

the truce with the bees, the uncovered queen,
swarm at the heart.

QUESTIONS FOR LAVINIA DICKINSON

> "... shortly after Emily's death... Lavinia discovered a collection of hundreds of poems. Beneath her hands lay her sister's life work, in unexpected profusion."
>
> JANE LANGTON

After your beloved sister was *Called Back*
and gone, did you roam her room
for hours, smoothing the long white gowns,
gathering the garments to fold
and pack away;

did some murmuring power instruct you,
or was it the mundane
reflex of grief
causing you to open the last
cherrywood drawer where you found
the stashed, locked box?

And you had the key Lavinia,
you had the key.
After you turned it,
did the stitched packets of words
tremble in your palms—

> *The embers of a Thousand Years*
> *Uncovered by the Hand—*

were you scorched
by their triumphant, necessary light?

A VISITOR TO HAWORTH PARSONAGE

From Mrs. Gaskell's "A Biography of Charlotte Brontë," *1857*

All was immaculate,
bare as an empty bowl.
Our shoes clattered on cold stone floors.
Like a pendant
Charlotte's own portrait hung
over the marble overmantel.

Into the parlour she appeared–
this living
embodiment of Jane,
diminuative   soundless

    gliding like a newborn bird,
the force of fiery life,
a creature destined

to roam the grey
tomb of a home where

the sisters' voices sang–spirits
blowing moor winds
through cracks in the window frames.

RENDEZVOUS WITH LIGHT

Thomas Wentworth Higginson, 1870

In the crowded Amherst parlor I stood
fingering the rim of my hat,

Anticipation unravelling into
those footsteps as if arriving from

some hidden, parallel air.
In blue and white, she appeared—

woman/gnome, she who'd once asked me if
her verses breathed.

What could I offer to someone
with lilies for hands. She touched me.

I bowed before her circumference,
her fiery mist unnerved me.

APPLIED LITERATURE

Too late for a hotel, an acquaintance offers us
this house high up in the village,
abandoned but for her brother's mattress
and chairs, the dust and grit of the Greek
island year sealing every surface, no heat
and the Cycladic wind like a creature rising lashing
and slapping the stone walls where we tried hard
to sleep, wind moaning (I finally decided)
like a grieving and venemous Heathcliff, beloved
book of my girlhood, and I with the chance to become
Catherine Earnshaw for one night as I pulled open
the split wood door into the howling darkness; my long, pale
nightgown billowing around my bare legs as I stumbled
outside–my moor–toward the one working place to pee.

AT THE GYM WITH THE BRONTËS

Briskly walking and never arriving,
I feel slightly silly,
my gaze bobbing under florescent light
as I try to read the pages of *Jane Eyre*
weighted down on the metal tray.
Behind it, flashing red tells me
if my heart is doing its work,
if I've lopped off the damage
from last night's pie,

though I'm certain Emily and Charlotte,
even Anne, never thought of calories as
they trod their restless moors,
what on earth would they say about
exercising a body where
there is no soul to expand it,
no hems grazed by dirt and gorse,
nor hairs wrestled and and undone
by a zealous wind while curlews swoop
and shriek in assent.

AT THE MALL CINEPLEX

Herded into the narrow aisles,
I can't help thinking of the Fox-Bay theater
on long Saturday afternoons;
the high school kids in burgundy blazers
ushering us into the hushed generous darkness
smelling of spilled popcorn
and thrumming with the promise
of a double feature, permission
to empty our boxes of Milk Duds
and JuJu Bees, our Good 'n Plenty
and tall cups of Hi-C,
the dark velvet drapery rolling open,
manuvered by careful, invisible hands,
while far away on the walls—the relief sculptures
of gnarled, windswept trees,
cliffs where a heroine might perch
awaiting her story.

AFTER WRITING THE POEM

The poet is left winded and warm, pacing
the platform, wooden slats creaking
under her steps as the true poem pulls away
from the station, the poem

   she would have caught if she'd been agile
   enough, brave enough to leap
   through the loud, steam-clogged air
   toward that country that spreads beyond silence.

THIS MORNING IS NOT A POEM

It will not heed
Emily's edict to *tell
it slant.*

No, this lake is too chiselled
cerulean, this June sky
practically shouting its light

with the wind, oh the wind
won't stop touching me
with its ravenous,

wordless breath.

EMILY DICKINSON AND EMILY BRONTË

Weren't we the consummate
breadmakers,

the Nobodies behind
Ellis Bell, anonymous.

In our kitchens, at our desks,
did you see souls at white heat—*no tremblers*

in the world's storm-troubled spheres,
a constancy of Hosts above us.

We Lit the Lamps—ourselves
went out—Sisters

(as it should be)
in Eternity now.

WOMEN POETS BEFORE ME

Some days I can almost hear
long skirts rustling–
the lanky one with the determined gait,
her cropped, autumn-hued hair shining,
the other with poppies in her hands,
white gown like drapery billowing into the other world
before she goes.
Not muses exactly–
reminders
of what survives–
creation's flames that gutter,
flare.

ANDREA POTOS is the author of three poetry collections: *Abundance to Share With the Birds* (Finishing Line Press, 2010), *Yaya's Cloth* (Iris Press, 2007) which received an Outstanding Achievement Award in Poetry from the Wisconsin Library Association, and *The Perfect Day* (Parallel Press, 1998). She has also received the James Hearst Poetry Prize from the *North American Review*, and the Sow's Ear Poetry Review Prize. Her poems appear widely in journals and anthologies in print and online, including: *Poetry East, Southern Poetry Review Women's Review of Books, Atlanta Review, Prairie Schooner, Rosebud, Poemeleon, Blue Fifth Review, Pirene's Fountain, Beloved on the Earth* (Holy Cow! Press), *Claiming the Spirit Within* (Beacon Press), *A Fierce Brightness* (Calyx Books), and *I Feel A Little Jumpy Around You* (Simon & Schuster). She works as a bookseller at A Room of One's Own Bookstore in Madison, Wisconsin where she lives with her husband, daughter and puppy.